How to Start
Trout Fishing

Other Benn Fishing Handbooks

Fly Tying for Beginners
GEOFFREY BUCKNALL

The Super Flies of Still Water
JOHN GODDARD

Fifty Favourite Nymphs
T. DONALD OVERFIELD

Fifty Favourite Dry Flies
T. DONALD OVERFIELD

Floatmaker's Manual
BILL WATSON

Manual of Sea Fishing Baits
HUGH STOKER

Other Benn Books of Interest

G. E. M. Skues: The Way of a Man with a Trout
T. DONALD OVERFIELD

Flytying Techniques: a full colour guide
JACQUELINE WAKEFORD

The Trout and the Fly
BRIAN CLARKE and JOHN GODDARD

Two Hundred Popular Flies and how to tie them
TOM STEWART

Taff Price's Stillwater Flies: Book 1

Poul Jorgensen's Modern Trout Flies and how to tie them

The Masters on the Nymph
eds. J. MICHAEL MIGEL and LEONARD M. WRIGHT JR

Gordon Mackie

How to Start
Trout Fishing

Ernest Benn Limited
London and Tonbridge

First published in 1980 by
Ernest Benn Limited
25 New Street Square, London EC4A 3JA
& Sovereign Way, Tonbridge, Kent, TN9 1RW
© Gordon Mackie 1980

Set, printed and bound in Great Britain by
Fakenham Press Limited, Fakenham, Norfolk

ISBN 0 510–22535–7 lib.
     0 510–22539–X p/b.

Preface

The fly fishing scene is an ever changing one. Just in the past 25–30 years the number and variety of trout waters has increased dramatically, resulting in far easier access, and at reasonable cost. Our knowledge of trout rearing, of the general behaviour of fish and of the food they eat is greater, and modern tackle is much superior to that used by our fathers and grandfathers. An angler taking up fly fishing today is very fortunate indeed, for he is in at the start of a golden era, a trout fisherman's paradise we might call it, the like of which was almost certainly undreamed of half a century ago.

For the newcomer, whether he is an angler already from some other branch of the sport or a complete beginner, it is most important that he may have access to the very latest information about tackle and techniques, and this is one of the main reasons that this new book is being introduced. You may find it different in some respects from what might be described as the 'standard' beginner's work, for I believe that fly fishing, to be truly rewarding, is only partly to do with 'hardware' such as rods, lines, reels, and the rest, and only partly to do with the techniques of casting and presentation.

These are the basics, and the beginner is likely to gain a reasonable command of such matters quite soon. One of the aims of the book is to help him to do this, but to be really successful and to obtain the maximum of enjoyment from the sport the fly fisher will also wish to explore some of the deeper mysteries beyond, such as an ability to 'read' water to know where trout are likely to be lying, when they will feed, and what they are feeding on; to assess the possibilities of a given piece of water and judge the best approach; to know how best to overcome, even to exploit, numerous minor difficulties such as might be caused by wind, current, sunlight, or the presence of trees or bushes.

It has been said that there is no short cut to success in fishing, and certainly there is no better way to learn than by experience, but a good 'primer' can eliminate much of the early trial and error, giving the budding fly fisher a head start and allowing his skills to develop more rapidly, and along the right lines.

Contents

This angler has played his fish direct on the line, not from the reel, and has the line trapped by his fingers as he nets the trout (Photo © Angling Times)

1 Introduction

I learnt my fly fishing from bitter experience, missing or losing or frightening fish after fish for weeks on end, wondering whether I would ever master problems which to me seemed quite insuperable. If only I had had a book to read which had explained, sympathetically, those difficulties which I was experiencing, then my fishing diary in that first season or two might have told a very different tale.

I know now that with the right sort of guidance a newcomer can catch fish from the outset, that after a dozen or so outings he may be a pretty competent performer, and that at the end of his first season he may well have achieved a highly satisfactory standard. But when I started I had no such guidance. I hesitated to seek advice from others for fear of betraying my inexperience. An acute awareness of my lack of knowledge was the greatest barrier to my gaining that knowledge. But little by little, simply by examining the reasons for my lack of success, and the faults which caused them, I started to catch a few fish, and that brought me that most vital ingredient – confidence.

From that point – I would then have been part way into my third season – life was crammed full of glorious angling adventures and I longed, every minute of my time away from the water, to be by some chuckling trout stream or drifting quietly in a boat over mysterious depths.

When I look through my diaries now I recall countless moments of breathless excitement, battles with great fish in which I seemed far removed from the realities of this world, so intense and thrilling were they. Sometimes the fish were landed, sometimes not, but the memory is as sharp whichever way the struggle ended.

One of these incidents took place late on a calm midsummer evening at Blagdon lake, nestling in a most beautiful valley a few miles south of Bristol. Three or four trout were cruising quite quickly near my position as I stood knee deep about ten yards from the shoreline. I could see the rise forms against the sunset glow as each one came within casting range, and I dropped the sedge fly on the water at what I judged to be the correct distance ahead of them. One of the trout took my fly with a sudden and vicious 'bang', jerking the rod point to the surface, but after a moment or two he came off. Then, as I was playing the second after another crash take and headlong dash towards the middle of the lake, I saw a trout of mammoth proportions quietly following my unfortunate victim as he plunged and cart-wheeled this way and that. Slowly I led my fish into the shallows. The water was warmer here and I knew he would soon tire, but I was all the while watching that monster, just praying that he would not be frightened away as I netted out the smaller fish.

It was difficult to see the outline of that huge trout, but he was swimming so close to the surface that the great head caused a distinct bow wave, and the dorsal fin scythed water, like that of a hungry shark. He looked all of two and a half feet in length, which would put his weight at something over the double figure mark.

The smaller trout scaled two pounds exactly, a silvery beauty and a good one by any standards, but for the moment I had lost sight of the big one. I had to hunt him down, for that trout would most likely be the largest I would ever see. The rise was over now, save for the occasional leap far out across the lake, but in the failing light I thought I saw a tiny movement out of the corner of my eye. It was no more than that, a minute ripple such as might have been caused by a moth fluttering briefly on the water. I cast out quickly, moving the fly slightly to simulate the scutter of a hatching sedge.

There was a leisurely heave in the surface and an unmis-takable fin and tail showed for an instant. I tightened cauti-ously and felt the kind of obstruction as when the fly touches a piece of weed Then the line started to move slowly through the water, and I felt sure it was my trout and that he was on. I struck hard into the fish, harder I expect than most good authorities would advise, and then I knew for certain.

There was an almighty pull and an angry boil as the surface erupted, great columns of spray pluming out for yards in all directions. The rod bucked as if it were a live thing and the reel fairly screamed. Far out over the lake a great shape seemed to hang for a moment in the air, then it jack-knifed, and plunged back into the water with a resounding smack.

The trout plummeted down through unknown fathoms towards the lake bed. I felt a dreadful juddering as the line snagged against some unseen peril, an old bridge perhaps, even the remains of a house in which people had lived a century and more ago. I dared not put on too much pressure, for the leader must have weakened during the struggle. Then, I could hardly believe my luck, the great trout was swimming towards me. I reeled in furiously and before I knew it he was almost at my feet, wallowing within two or three yards of the net.

I drew him nearer, but he saw me and summoned up sufficient strength for a final dash for freedom. I failed to slacken the line quickly enough and he jumped into the air, body twisting and turning against the afterglow of a summer sky. As he fell the leader snapped, the line whipping back on the recoil to drape forlornly from my shoulder.

I was shattered, spiritually and physically, drained of any strength or emotion. Happily, I have since landed many big trout, but have never again hooked anything approaching the weight of that enormous fish. Strangely though, as you will find, no matter how dreadful such experiences seem at the time, your enthusiasm the next day is in no way diminished.

We all have disasters. But there are occasions when everything seems to go right. One day, on a tributary of the Hampshire Avon, it looked as though I was in for a blank, for it was getting late and few trout were to be seen feeding. This is unstocked water where a pound fish is a good one and a two pounder quite a prize. I had reached the tail of a weir pool and was contemplating packing up, when I noticed what appeared to be a very small fish, probably a dace, dimpling the surface just above a raft of weed. I cast my fly in his direction, more for something to do than anything else, and had the surprise of my life. A big fish shot off across the current, then tore past me into a deep hole just downstream of my position. He kept trying to bury himself into a dense weedbed, but I held him hard and inside two minutes a bundle of fury was thrashing violently in the net. He scaled 2 lb 2 oz.

Looking up, I saw another minute disturbance in precisely the same spot. The performance was repeated exactly. Off went the trout in the same direction, then down into the same hole. Again I held the fish firmly as he struggled ferociously on the surface. The net strained as I lifted the trout ashore. This one went 3 lb 2 oz. Within fifteen minutes the day was transformed from a near certain blank into one to be remembered always.

---

2 How to Obtain Fishing

Before anybody begins to fish, he should be in possession of a Water Authority rod licence. This is a statutory requirement, applicable to most areas in England, no matter what kind of water he intends to fish, whether it be a pond or some tiny stream, or in 'free' waters such as may be found in or near some towns and cities.

Rod licences are issued by the Regional Water Authorities, whose addresses may be found in local telephone directories – see under 'Water'. Water Authorities assess the cost of licences individually by region, so this will vary according to the area in which you live. Usually, there is one licence to cover fishing for coarse fish, and a separate one for trout, salmon and sea trout. Juniors – often this means under the age of 16 years – may obtain licences at a considerable reduction in cost.

Exceptions to the rod licence laws exist only in a few areas. No rod licence is required to fish Scottish waters, while in the Republic of Ireland licences are issued only for salmon and sea trout fishing. It is advisable, of course, to ascertain whether a licence is required for your particular area.

While rod licences may be purchased direct from Regional Water Authority offices, anglers usually obtain them from 'agents'. These include most major tackle shops, some 'fishing' hotels, and occasionally an individual such as a fishery manager or river keeper. Your nearest tackle shop is likely to be the best bet. If for any reason they do not supply licences, they will let you know where they may be obtained.

A note of warning. Should you be found fishing without a rod licence on water where one is required, a bailiff appointed by the Water Authority is empowered to confiscate tackle, and may begin proceedings against the offender subject to his discretion. Having bought your licence, always ensure that you carry it with you when you go fishing. It's not much use telling the bailiff that you have one but have left it at home!

It is well worth getting to know your local bailiff. He can be a good friend, full of useful information, and you will find he is always pleased to help the beginner in any way he can. Most are very experienced fishermen with a deep understanding and love of the countryside. They know all the good fishing spots too.

Fishing Permits

The Water Authority rod licence does not entitle you to start fishing on private water. All fresh waters are owned by somebody, and it is necessary to obtain permission, usually in the form of another printed 'Permit', in all cases except some so-called 'free' waters. These free waters are normally controlled by the local council.

Fishing permits are usually issued by the individual fisheries. Some let season tickets only, and others, including most stillwaters, issue tickets by the day or part day. On stillwaters, these tickets may usually be obtained on site, either from the fishing lodge or from 'help yourself' points. Here, you simply follow the instructions, which may entail filling out a form and placing this together with your fee into an envelope, 'posting' it in the slot provided, and taking your ticket. Many lakes and reservoirs are controlled and managed by the Regional Water Authorities themselves.

In some cases, privately owned fisheries ask you to book tickets in advance by letter or telephone. The owner or manager will then send the tickets to you on receipt of the fee, or have them ready for you when you arrive at the water.

Fisheries will vary one from another as to the price, the number of permits issued in any one day, and in the method of payment. This may seem somewhat confusing, but conditions cannot be 'standard' throughout, for waters vary considerably in size, staffing arrangements and so on. It is very useful to get hold of a list of waters which let day tickets. These are published from time to time in most angling papers and journals, together with arrangements for booking, and are also likely to be available from Regional Water Authority offices. Advertisement columns, too, are well worth scanning with a view to finding suitable water. *Trout and Salmon*, *Trout Fisherman*, *Angling Times*, *Angler's Mail*, and several other publications, contain these, with details of how to apply. Tackle shops are always pleased to let you know fishery locations in their area, and in some cases may be agents for the fishery themselves and thus be able to supply your ticket.

Most large towns and cities have a local angling club, which in many cases own or rent trout waters for the fly fisherman. There is seldom any difficulty gaining membership, and often the subscription is relatively low. Enquiries locally will reveal the name and address of the club Secretary or Treasurer to whom applications may be made. Again, the tackle shop may be in a position to arrange your membership. Usually you will be issued with a map of the waters you are entitled to fish, and boundaries on river stretches are likely to be clearly marked with notice boards so that no confusion should arise.

NEVER BE AFRAID TO ASK FOR HELP OR INFORMATION. Tackle shops, especially, advise people like you and me every day on all manner of subjects. That's what they are there for, and also to supply any tackle you may need. I have always found them, and indeed any anglers I meet on the bank too, extremely friendly and helpful. There is a great spirit among fishermen, which applies to all branches of our sport, and I often think that if the world's affairs were run by anglers, there would be fewer problems generally. But maybe we would then have no time to go fishing, and it is those very problems from which many of us wish to escape!

Fishery Regulations

Before you decide to book your fishing, it is wise to check the methods which may be used on a particular water. While it is unlikely that you will be restricted to floating flies only, and this only on a very few of the most exclusive stretches, you may well find that the rules permit upstream fishing only, on rivers, or prohibit hooks above a certain size. Some fisheries allow all types of fly fishing, upstream or across and down, any size of lure at any depth, but others prefer you to use only representations of small aquatic insects and discourage searching the water downstream. Rules usually reflect the kind of opportunities for sport which a given water will provide, and the various methods are described in the following chapters (so don't worry if, at this stage of the book, you don't understand all the terms earlier in this paragraph).

You can certainly ask the fishery manager about recent results, and you will need to know all the rules which apply on that particular water. Fisheries are sometimes reluctant to pass on information as to stocking policies, however, and are unlikely to tell you dates on which restocking is taking place. You might be well advised not to ask about this, for you may be labelled as a fish-hog! Fishery managers do all they possibly can to ensure that good numbers of trout are present throughout the season, for those who can catch them, and few anglers want to kill completely 'tame' fish.

Your catch will be limited to a certain number of trout in any one day. It may be only two fish, or possibly as many as eight. This will vary according to the price and the sort of yield which a water can offer. On some fisheries, you can catch your limit, then buy another ticket and start again. But you may feel that if you take two or three fish you have had a pretty good day and are satisfied with that. Indeed, you will have done well, for the average number of trout taken per rod on some of our best known stillwaters is less than two fish per day.

Fishing Diary

Many fly fishermen keep a fishing diary, or at least some form of record of their catches. Fishing days are very precious, but the memory of them can quickly fade or become distorted as other days come and go.

A well maintained and accurate diary will provide invaluable information as the seasons pass, as well as enabling you to build up a clear picture of your own development as an angler.

You will probably be more successful too, for the diary will remind you that a certain fly or method was especially productive on a given water at a particular time of year; that fish come into condition sooner and feed more freely on one water than on another; that the evening rise usually begins

Date	Length	Location	Taken. Weight	Fly	Comments
Apr. 20th	11"	Usk. Town water		March Br.	This column is used to record details of
"	14"	" " "	1 lb 2 oz	"	weather, trout activity, fly hatches, taking
26th	9"	Box Brook. Beat 1		Greenwell	times. On the facing page is a record of
"	16"	" " "		"	other incidents, sketches of waters, fish
"	10½"	" " Beat 2	8 oz	P.T. Nymph	lies, etc., as well as monthly totals.
May 1st	16"	Cross Valley Lake	2 lb 1 oz	Butcher	
"	14½"	" "	1 lb 5 oz	Invicta	

in early June on this water, and the Mayflies start to hatch about May 20th on that; that trout rose madly in a particular tree-lined bay during the last week of April, when the wind from a certain quarter blew hundreds of Hawthorn flies onto the surface. While a beginner may develop fishing skills very quickly, this kind of information will furnish him with background knowledge, and a deeper understanding of the ways of trout and of the food they eat.

For my own diary I use a foolscap sized hard-backed ring binder, into which pre-punched sheets are clipped. The left hand page of the open log is devoted to statistics, and a space for general comments about weather conditions, fly hatches, etc. The right hand page I use for any other remarks, sketches, or month by month totals.

I record each trout caught on a separate line, estimating the length of those which have been returned to the water. Trout killed are carefully measured and weighed. Other fish, principally grayling or dace in my case, are entered after the trout for each day, but I only record the total number of these fish caught, rather than list each individually, with a note of any which were of exceptional weight.

At the end of each season I write a short summary, and total the number of fish caught by month and for the year. I calculate the average weight of trout taken, and total the flies on which they were caught. At the back of the book I keep a running total of 'big fish', those over 2 lb in my case (although 'big' on some waters may be $\frac{3}{4}$ lb and on others perhaps 3 lb). Here I include length, location, and fly pattern in each case.

Thus I have an accurate record of every fish I have ever caught, now over 7000 of which over 4000 have been trout. I know which flies have been most successful, and where and under what conditions they proved productive. I also have some wonderful material for reminiscence on winter evenings, and hopefully for old age, or when I can no longer throw a fly onto water.

3 Types of Trout Waters

Topography and Food Supply

The characteristics of a particular river or lake, such as its clarity, depth and rate of flow, and also its chemical value and other factors, are governed by the topography in a given area. Formations of rocks, soils, sandstones, chalk deposits and the like often make the conditions we find on one water completely different from those on another.

The level of alkalinity in a piece of water has a great bearing upon the kinds of plants and animal life which flourish there, as has the nature of the lake or river bed. Waters of high alkaline content (for example, those in chalk or limestone areas) are likely to provide an abundance of insect life and other food items, such as snails, crayfish and shrimps, while in more acid waters (such as are found in some moorland districts, and areas of peat) food may be in relatively short supply. This in turn largely determines the rate of growth of the fish which inhabit the water, so that a three year old trout, as an example, may reach 13 inches and weigh 1 lb where the food supply is rich, while those elsewhere may be only half that size or smaller.

Flow rate is a critical factor. A river which tears down the side of a hill, for example, is likely to contain little in the way of plant or insect life, simply because plants cannot put down roots there, nor can many of the aquatic creatures maintain position and become established. Any fish which live here will remain small, for even if they are able to find sufficient food to survive, the pace of the water may mean that considerable energy loss will result.

Trout Lies and Growth Rate

A trout must gain more energy from its food than it expends in obtaining it, if it is to put on weight and maintain condition. Hence it always selects areas in which the maximum amount of food can be obtained for as little effort as possible. In fast flowing rivers trout will lie away from the force of the current, behind rocks or in the 'cushion' in front of them, or in any areas of relatively slack water at the sides of the main flow, the 'undertow' beneath a weir fall, or in little bays along the river margin. Here they will find what food they can, only coming out into quicker water when the quantity of insects available there makes it worthwhile, as during a 'hatch' of flies. Fly hatches occur at intervals on many days in the season, especially in the spring and early summer, and the angler may then see flies floating on the water and trout rising to take them from the surface.

Trout which inhabit fast rivers, especially where these are of a more acid nature, clearly have a greater struggle for survival than those living in slower flowing streams where food is plentiful. Here, although the same law of energy gain/loss applies, and is equally critical to a trout's well being, the degree of urgency is less apparent, since food is more prolific and the amount of effort needed to obtain it is that much less.

Similarly, on stillwaters, although we are not concerned here with rapid flows, the trout's whole pattern of behaviour, where it feeds and when, and also its size and general condition, will depend upon its environment. Some of the hill lochs in Scotland, for example, are very deep, the cliff sides sometimes falling sheer to the lake bed. There may be little weed growth here, food is likely to be scarce, and the trout will generally remain small. By contrast, other lakes and reservoirs are relatively shallow, with heavy growths of water plants and plenty of food creatures to enable trout to grow quickly and survive in large numbers.

Between these extremes there is a whole range of trout waters which vary widely in character and general quality. Over the centuries certain fly fishing techniques have evolved which have been influenced by these con-siderations, and in the following pages we discuss individually the different kinds of water with which we are concerned, dividing them broadly into six types, their general character and the methods which are likely to be most suitable. Each is accompanied by a diagram showing typical areas in which trout may be found.

4 Large Lakes and Reservoirs

There is little doubt that in England more trout fishermen operate on reservoirs and large man-made lakes than on any other type of water, and it is largely because of the opening of so many new stillwater fisheries of this kind that there has been such a tremendous upsurge of interest in fly fishing. These lakes are stocked at intervals, usually with both brown and rainbow trout, to provide good sport throughout the season, and it is here that many beginners make their first tentative casts. Normally these waters are relatively shallow, and in places the angler can often wade a considerable distance out from the shoreline.

Towards the end of the book (chapter 12) you will find details of tackle, information which is valuable for the beginner. And at the ends of each of chapters 4 to 9 is a note about the basic tackle likely to be suitable for the various types of water discussed in those chapters. These are purely my own recommendations. The newcomer should not feel they are 'standard', for I would urge him to try out different tackle, seeking advice at the tackle shop and from other anglers, until he is sure he is using the gear that best suits his own individual requirements. You may in fact wish to refer to chapter 12, concerning tackle, or to chapter 10, which deals with natural and artificial flies, while you are reading this section of the book.

So Much Water!

On reaching the lakeside, the bank fisherman is immediately faced with an important decision. Where, in this vast expanse of water, should he begin to fish? The strength and direction of the wind is often a deciding factor, but the choice is seldom a simple one. If you select the windward bank, you have the wind behind your arm which makes for easier casting, and there is always the possibility that land bred flies are being blown onto the surface, attracting fish to the area. On the other hand, food items which remain on or beneath the surface are likely to drift with the current towards the opposite shore.

So either bank may be productive. I often start on the bank into which the wind is blowing, especially when it is

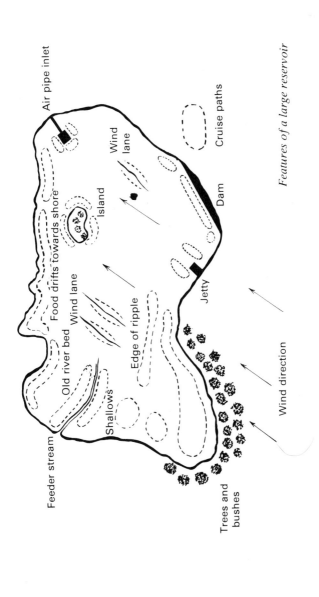

Air pipe inlet

Food drifts towards shore

Island

Wind lane

Wind lane

Old river bed

Feeder stream

Shallows

Edge of ripple

Dam

Jetty

Cruise paths

Wind direction

Trees and bushes

Features of a large reservoir

strong, and fish along the shoreline. Here, in the surf and lapping waves, there is often a large quantity of food. Casting out at about 30° from the bank, across the wind rather than directly into it, the line will soon 'belly' towards the shore and the flies will work sweetly, bobbing with the waves in a most attractive manner. The line should be kept relatively tight, however, so that you feel the takes, and it is important to be ready for trout which may grab the fly immediately it touches the water or while it is sinking.

Fishermen often make the mistake of assuming that trout are mostly to be found far out into the lake, whereas the best feeding grounds are usually in the shallower areas, sometimes of only a foot or two in depth. When approaching, it is always wise to fish carefully over these spots before wading out to cover deeper water. Cast ahead of you and to either side as you enter the water, remembering that trout are shy creatures and will be frightened if you cause too much disturbance. Start by making short casts so that you are not pitching beyond any trout feeding nearby.

The 'edge of the ripple', the line at which the wind ceases to play on the surface, leaving a calm area inshore, is always worth fishing carefully. This will apply when you are near the lee bank, or as the wind drops towards evening. If you are not catching fish, don't be afraid to keep on the move. Many bank anglers stay in the same place all day, 'planting' the landing net nearby to reserve their chosen spot. The thoughtful fisherman will seek out his trout rather than wait for them to come into his area. Mind you, if you are getting takes, then it will pay to stay put until such time as the fish go off the feed. Remember that trout are creatures of habit, and when the wind has remained in the same quarter for several days, they will have become accustomed to feeding in that area where most food is available. So if you go out on a windless day on which there is no indication of where the trout may be, consider the wind direction immediately prior to your visit. The fish will very likely be on the lookout for food in those same areas as in the recent past.

Lure Fishing

Early in the season a lure, which does not represent closely any insect but may resemble a small fish, on a hook size of perhaps 8 or larger, may be the most effective type of pattern to use. The method of fishing the lure is usually to cast out and retrieve by gathering in the line with the free hand, either onto the water on into a special line-tray strapped to the waist. There is room for a lot of experiment with a lure. You may begin by retrieving at speed, stripping the line quickly through the rings, the lure swimming rapidly just beneath the surface. If this is not successful, you can allow the lure to sink to a depth of perhaps 4 ft to 5 ft and retrieve more slowly, or sink it deeper and inch it back so gradually that the process takes several minutes. You can make the lure move in all manner of different ways, from short jerks at long intervals to quick darts of a foot or more in rapid succession. Keep experimenting until you discover the depth at which the trout are feeding, and what manner of presentation is most successful at the time.

You should always work the lure by pulling on the line with the free hand rather than by lifting the rod. Keep the rod low, horizontal with the water or perhaps with the tip at a slightly higher level than the butt section. This will ensure that you are always in a position to tighten at once by raising the rod point the moment you feel a fish or see a disturbance near your fly. When you tighten, do it quickly but at the same time gently, so avoiding a break, and you should make sure that the free hand is holding the line firmly as you raise the rod tip. If you let go of the line, the strike-power of the rod will be greatly reduced, and you may fail to set the hook firmly in the fish's jaw.

As the season progresses, you may find that lure fishing no longer brings results. Trout may now be more selective as they become less ravenous and a wider variety of food becomes available. Then you are likely to find a smaller wet fly or nymph pattern more productive. These imitate the water born flies more closely, and while quick retrieve or stripping methods will sometimes pay, I have found that the best results are usually achieved by fishing the flies more slowly, sometimes very slowly indeed.

Flies are often fished in 'teams', two or three or more on the leader, one on the point and the others attached by means of 'droppers', short pieces of nylon tied to the main leader. The method of tying droppers is described in chapter 12. The advantage of presenting 'teams' is that you offer the fish a wider choice and you do so at different depths. To fish the flies slowly and yet fish them near the surface, it may be necessary to apply special grease to the leader in order to make that section or sections float. To make the leader sink, rub the nylon with a mixture of Fuller's Earth and household detergent or with soft mud.

It is not possible in this book to explore the subject of flies in great detail. The angler will develop confidence in certain patterns, and possibly he will devise and tie his own in time. But in the early days, he will be well advised not to get too involved in the 'mystique' which surrounds this subject. Often, the choice of fly is just a matter of individual preference. There is no such thing as a fly which will not catch fish, and likewise there is no universally successful one. Having said that, a beginner will certainly wish to study natural and artificial flies if he is keen, and I would suggest that he obtain one of a number of excellent books devoted to the subject, some of which I recommend in the section headed 'Further reading'. Throughout this book, however, reference will be made to certain flies seen on and about the waters, and in chapter 10 I give lists of the more common species and also many of the artificial flies which are commonly used by anglers.

Big Lake Tactics

I seldom use anything other than a floating or slow sinking line, varying the length of the leader from about 8 ft to perhaps 12 ft, depending on conditions, wind especially. But there is no doubt that a fast sinking line is very useful on occasion, to reach the depths, particularly in low temperatures early in the season or on hot days in mid-summer, at which times the trout tend to seek deeper water. I would advise the beginner to start with a leader point of reasonable strength, say 7 lb breaking strain. This will allow him a margin should he tighten too hard or fail to let a big trout run. The leader is not as likely here to foul on some obstruction or get caught up in dense weed as on some other waters, and one of the main considerations is to give the fish sufficient freedom on his first dash to avoid a break.

Playing a trout is a matter of give and take. Keep the rod point up, and allow him to take out line at the start – usually he will run towards the middle of the lake – and then tighten gradually. As he weakens put on more strain, winding line back onto the reel, but always be ready for another run. If the fish jumps out of the water, give him slack line by dropping the rod point immediately, or he may break the nylon, or throw the hook with an aerial twist or as he falls back into the water.

When you have recovered your line and have complete control, the beaten fish laying beneath the rod point, you can slip your net and put it into the water so that the meshes and supports are completely submerged. Then draw the fish smoothly over the net and lift him out.

When fishing from a boat, the basic techniques will be much the same. You may decide the approximate distance from the bank you wish to fish and allow the wind to drift the boat parallel with the shore. In a high wind, a drogue, acting as a brake in the water behind the boat, will ensure that it does not travel too quickly. Or you may wish to anchor off shore, casting inland to take advantage of those food concentrations mentioned earlier. A useful tip is to fish any areas where the wind causes an unusual pattern on the surface, such as 'wind lanes', taking the form of long, narrow strips of calmer water, or the edges of choppy areas. You may notice other strange currents and eddies, such as near islands or promontories of land. They are all worth fishing, as are inlets of feeder streams, along the dam wall, near jetties which jut out into the lake, and areas where submerged air pipes cause the surface to bubble.

Sometimes there will be a general rise, in which trout cruise about taking flies from the surface. They may sip the flies down quietly, or roll like porpoises or take with a wallop, depending largely upon the species of insect being taken. Some flies, like the midges, hang for a while from the surface film before hatching. Others, such as sedges, which are relatively large moth-like insects, flop and scutter about causing great excitement among the trout. You may then fish a dry fly, especially designed to float on the water. Watch the path of a cruiser and try to judge when and where to drop your fly. Let it sit there until the fish has either taken or passed it by. A slight twitch will sometimes attract the trout's attention.

The key to success, on lakes or elsewhere, is an open minded attitude and thoughtful approach, rather than mere conformity.

Basic Tackle for Large Lakes

$9\frac{1}{2}$–10 ft rod, middle to tip action

No. 7–9 double taper or forward taper floating line, possibly a sinker for fishing at depth

20–30 yards of backing line

10 ft tapered leader, point 6–7 lb b.s.

---

5 Smaller Stillwaters

Many stillwaters have been formed by the digging out of
pools along the course of an existing waterway. Some may
be only an acre or two in extent, or in character more like a
wide impounded river than a lake. A variety of other man-
made ponds and gravel pits may fall into this category.

Conditions here, although similar in some ways to those
on large lakes and reservoirs, are likely to be different in
certain important respects. Some will be deep at the sides,
possibly with shallow areas in the middle. Many are shel-
tered by trees, and often there is quite dense fringe vegetation or heavy growths of sedges along the margin. In some
cases there is even a distinct flow of water from the feeder
stream which drifts considerable quantities of food into the
lake.

Concealment

Trout often cruise to a lesser extent here, over limited areas
of perhaps 5–10 yards of water. You may even see fish
feeding in a fixed position, especially where water enters the
lake or at the outlet, or near weedbeds and beneath overhanging trees and branches. I find these small waters
intensely exciting to fish. One of the most vital con-
siderations is to remain hidden as far as you can from your
quarry. If you conceal yourself among bankside herbage
and keep still for a time, you may see the trout cruising
about as they feed, provided the light conditions are favour-
able. You may even be able to see the trout's mouth open
and close as it takes an insect, and spot flies hatching from

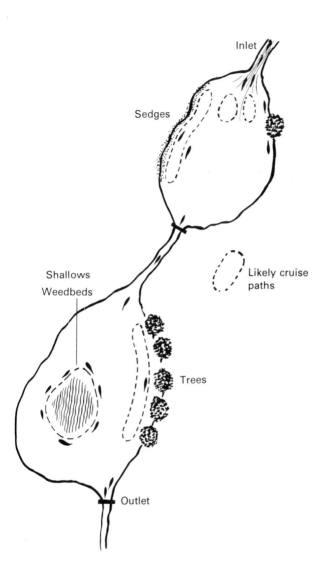

Features of a typical small stillwater

the surface film. The cruise path is plotted, the correct depth can be judged accurately by sight in the case of fish taking sub-surface food, and you can thus choose a fly pattern of sufficient weight to reach his position. In some conditions, polarised glasses are very useful in this kind of fishing, for by reducing reflected surface glare they enable you to spot fish which may not be visible to the naked eye.

While we rely to some extent on the law of averages when fishing on big lakes for unseen fish, here we are hunters, stalking and scheming the downfall of individual trout. As the fish approaches, we drop our fly a few yards ahead of him, having judged the correct line and depth. If he sees your fly there is every chance that he will take it. Your nerves are at peak tension and your hand shakes as the mouth opens, but you should wait until it closes on the fly before tightening. Truly, this is fascinating sport.

Shrimp imitations are often deadly on these waters, as are 'buzzer' nymphs of appropriate size and colour. If the trout are not interested in these, it often pays to change down to a smaller nymph, perhaps on hook size 12 or 14. The use of lead or copper wire in the construction of the fly helps you to get it down quickly to the fish's level.

Strong hatches of fly occur from time to time on some of these waters, in which you can see insects emerging from the surface and taking to the air. The trout may then feed from the surface, giving the angler a chance of a good bag on dry fly. If there is a high wind, land bred flies such as Alders or Hawthorn flies in spring, or Crane flies (Daddy longlegs) and moths in summer, and many other insects, may be blown onto the water. These small waters are not normally as universally windy places as are larger sheets of water, however, and in the more confined area trout are less inclined to congregate in one part of the lake or another. Even so, the point at which the water enters the lake is a well known hot spot, and in warm sunny conditions they like to take up lies in shaded areas, beneath overhanging trees perhaps, or along a sedgy margin. Here, they may pick up such titbits as caterpillars, beetles, spiders, ants and other insects.

Surface ripple, while it can reduce your chances of spotting fish, does have the advantage that they cannot see you as clearly, and you can thus fish at closer range. Never disregard cover completely, however, for in my experience

A nice fish for this early season boat angler
(Photo © Angling Times)

those who make use of bushes, reeds, etc. to shield their presence are usually the most consistently successful anglers.

Tackle and Tactics

In most cases I prefer to use a floating line with a relatively long leader, perhaps between 10 ft and 15 ft. Trout here are likely to be ultra shy, especially in sunny conditions and where the water is hard fished. Modern plastic coated fly lines can cause considerable shadow, and are likely to be very visible as they flash through the air and when they lie on the water. Some feel that a slow sinking or sink-tip line is less visible to trout, and this may well be true, as might the view that colour is an important factor. I have yet to prove either theory to my own satisfaction, but they are well worth further experiment.

Lure stripping techniques are not usually as productive on small stillwaters, and may indeed be frowned upon by the management or by other anglers because of the possibility that they alarm trout, putting them off the feed. More often, anglers use smaller flies of the wet fly type, or imitative nymphs and dry flies. It is best to make enquiries about which methods are considered most suitable, for in fishing we do tend to be a bit sensitive on such matters. Fishermen must always observe the rules laid down for a particular fishery, otherwise a good deal of embarrassment may result. In the chapter on angler behaviour (page 62) we examine this subject in greater detail.

Some of the trout in the waters which I know are huge, up to 20 lb or so. One fishery manager has successfully reared rainbow trout considerably in excess of this weight, and very soon someone is likely to catch one of 30 lb, or more. Just imagine the excitement, fear even, that you feel as you watch one of these monsters on the feed. Where fish of this size are a possibility, stouter nylon is of course advisable, perhaps of 10 lb breaking strain or more. Some of the modern, super tough nylons will allow you to fish this strength yet at the same time use a leader of reasonable diameter.

The basic techniques of playing and landing trout apply to all types of water, as described in the last chapter. But as I have already mentioned, on smaller lakes and ponds it is especially important to keep as still as you can, certainly avoiding any sudden movements, and to remain hidden as far as it is possible.

Chains of small lakes are sometimes intersected by quite fishable streams. If your ticket entitles you to fish in these, don't just ignore them as most anglers do. I once caught the biggest trout of the day at Avington, in a tiny brook, at a place where it was about three yards wide. Often such streams are full of little native born trout, and big escapees from the main pools may sometimes be found there.

Each season more and more of these small lakes are becoming available for public fishing on day ticket. We can now 'fish around' far more easily than was the case just ten years or so ago, broadening our experience on a wide variety of different fisheries.

Basic Tackle

The same outfit that was recommended for large lakes will probably be suitable here, although you may wish to fish with slightly lighter tackle.

$8\frac{1}{2}$–9 ft rod, middle to tip action
No. 6–7 double taper floating line
15 yards of backing line
10–15 ft tapered leader, point 4–5 lb b.s.

6 Moorland Streams

In their upper reaches, many of our major 'rain fed' rivers provide glorious small stream trout fishing. Over the centuries, direct rainfall 'run-off' has cut numerous channels in the hillsides. These soon increase in size as they join forces with others to form more substantial streams.

If you look at a large scale map of any moorland region, of Dartmoor perhaps, or the Welsh hills or Scottish highlands, it will be noticed that the watershed of most river systems appears as an intricate tapestry of minor brooks or burns. Many of these contain trout, lots of trout, yet the streams are often very lightly fished, if at all.

Here, flows are likely to be relatively quick, between granite or limestone rocks. The bed will be made up of boulders, which in places may have been broken down into small stones. As a rule, silt and fine gravel will be confined to areas unaffected by the scouring of fast water. Some of the aquatic insects commonly found elsewhere may be unable to survive in such conditions, but others, such as the Stoneflies, are well adapted to life here. Caddis flies, or Sedges, water snails, shrimps, and the larvae of such upwinged flies

31

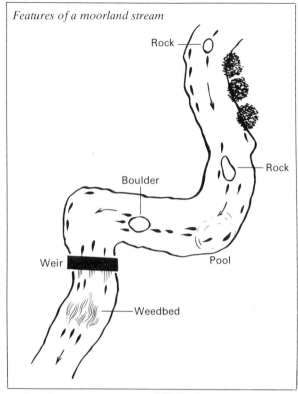

Features of a moorland stream

Rock

Rock

Boulder

Pool

Weir

Weedbed

as the March Brown and Blue Winged Olive may flourish too. We examine the subject of flies in some detail in chapter 10 (page 47).

If you examine the underside of stones along the edge of the stream, you may be surprised by the quantity and variety of creatures you can find. But while trout may grub among the stones, and even move them or turn smaller ones over, they generally depend upon the current to bring food items to them as they lie in fixed or semi-permanent positions. There is often much competition for food in heavily populated streams, and the amount which drifts with the current is at times fairly limited. In fast flows, trout may also expend a lot of energy in obtaining food, so that while they are usually fit and strong, and numerous, they are likely to be small, averaging perhaps little more than 4 oz to 6 oz.

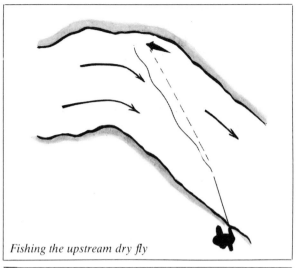

Fishing the upstream dry fly

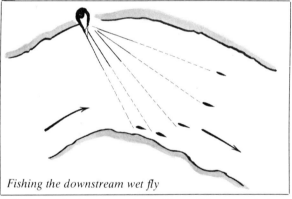

Fishing the downstream wet fly

But what glorious sport this is. You will hear much about the 'superior' fishing to be had on other waters, and the monsters which are caught on some lakes, but for me this small stream angling is as near as you can get to 'real' fishing. The streams are so completely natural, and the trout are wild, spawned on the clean gravels or in some little sidestream nearby.

The methods normally employed here are 'dry fly' – the angler casting a floating fly upstream or up and across, so that it drifts down on the surface over a riseform or a likely spot, and 'wet fly' – in which one or more flies, especially

33

designed to penetrate the surface, are fished submerged by casting across the current and allowing the flow to carry them downstream and across the river to a point below the angler's position.

In dry fly fishing the trout is usually seen to take by the tell-tale rise. With the wet fly method you more often feel the pull on your line, which is kept relatively tight. Skilled wet fly fishermen can 'work' the fly by manipulation of the line with the free hand, making it swim or hang attractively in the current. By slackening line tension you can cause the fly to sink an inch or two as it drifts unchecked with the stream; tightening the line or pulling on it will make the fly move across current and lift towards the surface. As soon as a rise is seen, or the slightest tug felt, the fisherman should tighten smartly, yet without violence, by raising the rod tip while holding the line firmly with the free hand. These little trout take like lightning and eject the fly the instant they discover it to be something other than a real insect.

Wading will often help you to keep out of sight and to cast to all parts of the stream, but do be careful. Try to cause as little disturbance as possible by wading SLOWLY. It pays to stand quite still for periods of several minutes, just watching the water for indications of feeding trout. It is surprising how close fish will come to your position if you have given them no cause for alarm.

Trout are often so numerous that you are likely to be covering fish wherever you cast your fly, but especially productive spots are behind, or in front of, major obstructions such as rocks; the slacker water at the sides of the main flow; smooth, shallow pool-tails; in quiet pockets along the bank, and beneath overhanging bushes.

While many prefer to use small, imitative fly patterns, trout are usually far from selective on moorland streams, sometimes taking almost any fly you care to offer. A high work-rate pays dividends here and a cautious approach is essential, as is a quick reaction to any sign of a take.

Basic Tackle

7–7½ ft rod, middle to tip action
No. 4–5 double taper floating line
5–10 yards of backing line
8–9 ft tapered leader, point 2–3 lb b.s.

7 Major Rain Fed Rivers

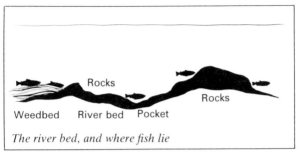

Rocks

Rocks

Weedbed   River bed   Pocket

The river bed, and where fish lie

The main difference between the streams flowing down the hillside and the parent river in the valley is one of size. Some of our major rain fed rivers are very wide indeed, perhaps up to 40 yards, or more, and in places quite impossible for the average angler to cast across. They often run fast and deep as well, and early in the season or after heavy rainfall can present a frightening picture, the river sometimes rising to a point where all the debris along the banks, even bushes and trees, come hurtling downstream, swept helpless on the boiling torrent.

Levels fluctuate considerably during the fishing season and the water may run brown on occasion. Before setting off for a weekend, and most of my outings to this kind of river are to the Usk in Monmouthshire or the Devonshire Torridge and Exe, I often make enquiries of friends living locally, or the nearest tackle shop, as to the state of the water. Mind you, I usually make the trip anyway, except when the river is in severe flood, for often a little colour or a slight rise in level can be conducive to good sport. This is particularly the case after a long period of drought in which the water has been so low as to make the fish especially shy or disinclined to feed in the high temperatures.

There is generally a mass of fly life on these rivers, and the trout often rise well. Sometimes dry fly fishing will be the more effective method, but often the wet fly will pay better dividends. This depends largely upon the water conditions prevailing at the time. Fishing wet fly across and downstream in areas of broken water is usually the more productive method early in the season, and in low water conditions at high summer. In the evening, however, you may do better

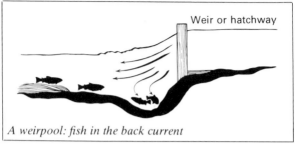

A weirpool: fish in the back current

on the smooth 'flats' with a dry fly. When the water is high and fast flowing after rain, areas of more steady water at the edges, or slower eddies and backwaters, may yield the most fish. Fishing the main current can be very rewarding during a heavy hatch of flies. March Browns, for example, emerge in short bursts during the middle part of the day in late March and throughout April on some rivers. You will learn to detect the signs quite soon, and discover the best spots to fish in given conditions. Two or three splashy rises in the quicker water during April immediately registers 'March Brown' in my mind; the same signs at evening in the summer may indicate that the fish are beginning to feed on Sedges. Often, of course, I am wrong. The former might be an indication that Stoneflies are on the water – the latter that grass moths or crane flies are being taken. But fishing is always a puzzle, even to the most experienced, and half the fun is trying to work out such problems.

It is often necessary to make relatively long casts on these big rivers, and even then trout seem to have the annoying habit of continually rising just out of reach. In low water you may be able to wade out to cover them, but always do so with extreme caution. The rocks are often slippery, the water will be deeper than it looks from the bank, and the currents can be deceptively strong.

The Problem of Drag

You will find on most stretches that currents vary a good deal as to pace and flow direction, even within a limited area. The presence of boulders on the riverbed, or weed growths, and constantly varying depths, create quick runs, small areas of slower water, backwaters, and deflections of currents. As we have seen, trout usually select the slacker

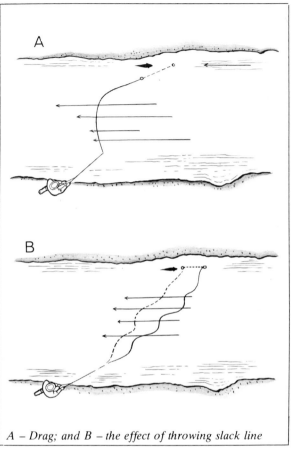

A – Drag; and B – the effect of throwing slack line

areas in which to feed, and the intervening fast water, between you and the fish, can cause a problem which is well known to all river fly fishermen – drag. This occurs when the water causes the line to 'belly' in the faster, intervening current, dragging your fly across the slower run beyond. Drag can frighten your fish, which is not used to seeing flies behave in such an unnatural manner.

To overcome this problem, try to cast plenty of 'slack' line, for clearly the current will take longer to belly a loose line than a tight one, and your fly will float naturally for a moment or two longer before it begins to drag, hopefully long enough to cover your trout properly. To cast slack line

I find it best to strip a yard or two more line off the reel than I actually need to reach the fish, and to throw it out high, with the rod hand at shoulder height, aiming at a spot perhaps 6 feet or more above the water. When the line is extended over the stream, I allow it to recoil to some extent by checking the forward movement of the rod, and fall in loose coils upon the water, at the same time lowering the rod to about waist height. In a particularly awkward drag situation it is sometimes necessary to place the fly right 'on his nose', for it may only be possible to achieve an inch or so of natural drift before the fly is whisked away, even as your trout is opening his mouth to take. Small wonder that strong language is not unknown on the riverbank!

Gaining access to most moorland streams and major rain fed rivers presents little problem as a rule. Local enquiry will reveal how you may obtain your permit.

Basic Tackle

9 ft rod, middle to tip action, or 'through' action with a little more play in the butt section

No. 7 double taper floating line, or possibly sink-tip for deeper wet fly fishing

15 yards of backing line

10–12 ft tapered leader, point 3–4 lb b.s.

8 Chalkstreams

The Classic Waters

These rivers are to be found mainly in central Southern England, in Hampshire and parts of Wiltshire, Berkshire and Dorset. There are also a few in other counties, such as Yorkshire and Kent. Chalkstream fishing is the most highly prized and expensive branch of our sport. Beginners seldom learn their craft on these rivers initially, more often taking up chalkstream fishing after having spent their early days or years on waters of different character. Access is not as easily

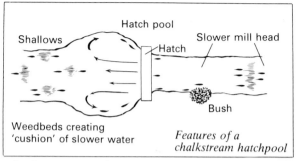

Features of a chalkstream hatchpool

(Labels within diagram: Hatch pool, Shallows, Slower mill head, Hatch, Bush, Weedbeds creating 'cushion' of slower water)

gained as to waters elsewhere, although more stretches are now open to season booking, and through town angling clubs, than was the case a few years ago.

The names of such streams as the Itchen, Test, Avon and Kennet are famed throughout the world, wherever people fish for trout with a fly, partly because so many of the fishing 'classics' were written by chalkstream anglers, who had the time to devote to their sport and a skill with words which rivals the very best in English literature. Works such as *A Summer on the Test*, by J. W. Hills, *Where the Bright Waters Meet*, by Harry Plunket-Green, and the prolific writings of G. E. M. Skues, F. M. Halford, more recently Oliver Kite, C. F. Walker and many others, paint a glorious picture indeed.

Do not be misled, however, into believing that chalkstream fishing is necessarily the most rewarding kind of fishing to be had. I fish chalkstreams regularly, and also rough rivers, brooks and stillwaters. Usually I catch more fish on rivers elsewhere, and those on stillwaters are often larger. I've often tried to put my finger on the real reason why chalkstreams are considered by many to be superior from the point of view of angling enjoyment, but really I cannot. Perhaps it has to do with the general environment, the lush beauty of these valleys and the flower-decked water meadows, the crystal clear streams with their brilliant green water plants. For me, there is certainly a feeling of utter peace and serenity about the riverside which I never experience to quite the same degree on other waters. Results seem to matter less than the sheer joy and tranquillity of just being there. But that is how I feel now, after many happy angling days. The beginner looks for incident, adventure, and hopefully a good bag of trout as well.

These streams rely very little upon surface run-off caused by direct rainfall, but upon the springs which issue from the porous chalk. Chalk hills act rather like a sponge in that they soak up and retain rain water, and when the level of water contained in them is sufficient, it pumps out of springs located in the river bed. The level of water in the river itself varies very little, and is always absolutely clear and free from impurities at source. It can pick up impurities as it flows down the valley, of course, and sometimes a limited amount of surface water from roads or sloping land nearby, but generally the rivers run clear and at roughly the same level all season.

Chalkstream Wrinkles

Weed growths are very dense, so much so that regular cutting takes place to enable us to fish, and many species of upwinged flies can flourish here in ideal conditions. The method of fishing is almost invariably by upstream casting, either with dry fly or imitative nymph patterns. In the clear water conditions trout are best approached from the rear of their position. Concealment is absolutely vital, and delicate presentation necessary so as not to scare the fish. Another reason why downstream fishing may be largely unproductive is that 'reading the water', so as to know roughly where trout are likely to be feeding, is extremely difficult in most stretches. Chalkstreams run a relatively straight course as a rule, the flow more evenly distributed from bank to bank. Seldom will you see a boulder, or even a stone of any size, the bed usually being made up of fine gravel or, in the slower reaches, silt.

The trout themselves are likely to be spread over the whole river, rather than in clearly defined areas as on other streams, and there are few stretches which run at any great pace. Furthermore, there is usually much less competition for food, since it is generally available in abundance. Thus the fish have the best of both worlds – plenty of food, and large areas of relatively slow flowing water in which to lie with a minimum expenditure of energy. Of course, competition is greater on those lengths which contain large numbers of grayling. These fish are present in many rivers, especially perhaps the Avon and Wylye in Wiltshire, providing some excellent fly fishing towards the end of the

Gordon Mackie nets a good trout on a Wessex chalkstream (Photo © Graham Swanson)

season. Indeed, I have caught grayling on dry flies in every month of the year. While I welcome the sport they offer, there is no doubt that trout grow more rapidly, and have a better overall condition factor, in waters where no grayling exist.

Although good chalkstream trout may lie in all sorts of unexpected places, there are certain spots which they seem especially to favour. Beneath footbridges, at the tails of weedbeds or in the 'cushion' in front of them, alongside walls or camp-sheathing, in backwaters such as are formed by the fast flow of a weir or hatch pool; always look, too, in the little carriers or sidestreams, which run out of the main river to join it again farther downstream.

Often there is little shelter from the wind in these wide valleys, and sometimes few trees beneath which you can take cover in the rain. But it is often in these very conditions that sport is at its best. Flies sometimes hatch in vast numbers in unsettled weather, and trout may then be seen rising everywhere. As elsewhere, the best of the daytime fishing is usually to be had during May and early June; thereafter, until the latter part of August, sport may be best at late evening, after the sun has gone over the hill; then in September the daytime fly hatches return as the evenings draw in, giving sport which is almost, though seldom quite, as hectic as in the springtime.

The ability to cast a slack line to overcome drag is useful on these streams, accurate and delicate presentation is usually very important, and the most vital consideration of all is an extremely cautious approach. On many streams your trout may continue rising even though you have cast to him a dozen times. On a chalkstream he may well stop feeding at the first or second chuck.

Basic Tackle

$8\frac{1}{2}$ ft rod, middle to tip action
No. 5–6 double taper floating line
10 yards of backing line
10–12 ft tapered leader, point 3–4 lb b.s.

---

9 Lowland Brooks

In this section we consider those streams which meander this way and that through low lying pasture land. There are many of these in various parts of the British Isles. They may be relatively slow flowing, often with alternate shallows and pools, the water usually tinged with colour, or distinctly brown, and they are sometimes considered to offer rather poor trout fishing. Don't you believe it, at least until you have tried for yourself.

I learned my fishing on a little stream in this category, the Box brook on the Wiltshire/Somerset border near Bath, and while it was overhung by bushes, the banks steep and

The much-neglected art of concealment (Photo © Graham Swanson)

sheer in places, and the pools contained the debris of many winters, it gave me hour upon hour of exciting sport and sometimes a catch of twenty or more trout in a day. Yet few others fished here. For a year or more I could find no way to cast a fly without getting my fly and leader entangled in the foliage, but I caught fish by 'dapping', simply lowering the fly onto the water over the trout's nose. You have to creep and crawl, peeping through the reeds for feeding fish, easing the rod between the branches, and you get stung by nettles and scratched by thorns, but this is hunting in its truest sense, and tremendous fun. Although I have moved on to other waters now, I hold treasured memories of those golden early days on the old 'Box'.

I discovered that by getting down the bank and standing in the water I could make short horizontal casts, and by wading slowly I could fish to many of the spots which were inaccessible before. As I moved forward, little trout would shoot upstream or down causing bow-waves, alarming others as they went, but as I stood motionless and waited I would soon see them begin feeding once more.

Fly pattern is not usually of major importance. I remember I used a Coch-y-Bonddu only one spring, and a Black Gnat the next; then I tried others, a Greenwell's Glory, a Tup's Indispensable, and Iron Blue. They all

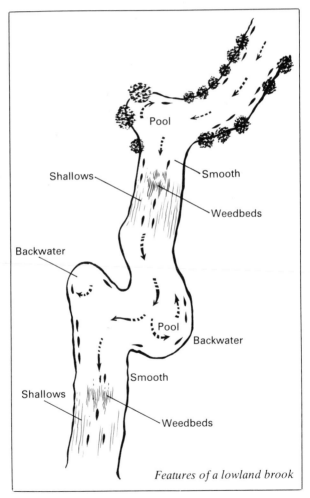

Features of a lowland brook

caught fish and the few others who fished the same water caught fish too, on flies which I had never heard of and looked nothing like my own. I talked to these fishermen, discovering what length of leader they used and its breaking strain; I heard of line grease to keep the line afloat, and fly floatants, and of a fungus called amadou to dry the fly when it became sodden; of weighted flies and fuller's-earth, and the use of 'droppers'. I learned by talking to them, and by reading books, and most of all from my own experiences.

Fish Location

Trout are not always easy to locate on these streams. When they are rising, of course, there is no problem, but often they are not. If you know the river well, having fished it for a number of years, you have a good idea of where it is best to fish, but rivers vary a good deal in character, and a new-comer may well fish for much of the day without a touch simply because he is not covering the trout.

In the early part of the season, from opening day until perhaps the end of April or early May, the trout tend to remain in the deeper pools of slow to moderate flow. They often lie deep down, coming into mid-water or near the surface only when there is a sufficient hatch of flies. There may be good fly hatches for many days, however, before they venture to rise and take them from the surface. Much will depend upon water conditions. If the river is high and coloured still from the winter rains they may not rise at all until it clears and falls to near normal spring height. Low temperatures may keep fish down in the early days, too. Often they will congregate in slow water near the banks, especially in backwaters, where some are likely to remain all season.

As the season advances, trout become more and more inclined to take up lies above and below the pools, in the broken water and shallow runs, and in bends where the flow is concentrated, funnelling the bulk of the insects into the area. In hot summer weather, trout seek shaded spots beneath trees and bushes, and well oxygenated areas of rough, broken water. They will often lie in quick water which is barely deep enough to cover their backs, and in the little pockets formed by water plants.

I like to locate and cast upstream to rising fish, but when

there is no rise it becomes necessary to 'fish the water' with a dry fly or sub-surface nymph. Wet fly fishing is productive at times, especially in broken water, and fishing a weighted nymph in the pools may bring results when trout are hard to locate.

Fishing the Deep Nymph

One of the difficulties of deep nymphing is detecting the take, for a trout will often take and eject your fly without any indication that he has done so. In slow flowing pools it is unlikely that you will feel a pull, and in cloudy water you can seldom see the fish themselves. I find the best way is to grease the butt section of the leader quite heavily so that it floats and acts as a 'sighter'. Judge the depth you wish the remainder of your nylon to sink and treat this section with fuller's-earth or soft mud. This will ensure that it sinks without hindrance. The nymph should be heavy enough to get it down to the required level quickly. Watch the greased section intently for any sign of movement, of slight acceleration or deviation from its natural drift, and when you see any indication that a fish has taken the fly, or even sense that it may have done, tighten instantly. You cannot tighten too quickly in deep nymphing, but you will lose many fish because you have failed to set the hook quickly enough.

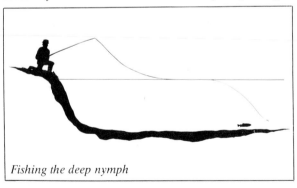

Fishing the deep nymph

I find in my own case that the highest proportion of catches to takes is achieved with a dry fly; next comes lightweight nymphing just under the surface, third downstream wet fly; and deep nymphing, at depths of four feet or more, a poor fourth. In fact I estimate that I fail to detect

46

nine takes out of every ten while nymph fishing for unseen
trout. Where the fish is clearly visible, however, my average
is almost as high as with a dry fly. Try all these methods for
yourself, and fish the way which suits you best in the given
conditions.

Basic Tackle

7–7½ ft rod, middle to tip action
No. 4–5 double taper floating line
5–10 yards of backing line
8–9 ft tapered leader, point 2–3 lb b.s.

---

10 Natural and Artificial Flies

The subject of flies can be the most complicated of all for
the beginner. It is fishermen and fly tyers who have made it
so, rather than Nature herself. If you go into a tackle shop
and look at the display of flies for sale, numbering hundreds
perhaps, or examine the contents of another angler's fly
box, even read some of the books devoted to the subject,
you may be a good deal more confused than you were
before.

This is one matter in which I would advise the beginner
not to be influenced over much by the views of others. Go to
the water, watch the natural insects hatching and search for
underwater creatures among the plants and stones, examine
them, and *then decide for yourself what you want your
artificial flies to look like*. Then, when you go to the shop,
choose the flies which you feel most nearly resemble those
you saw at the waterside.

You learn about flies by studying the natural insects. If
you can identify them by comparing them with the photo-
graphs in John Goddard's *Trout Fly Recognition*, or some
other work, so much the better. Note the character of the
water from which the various kinds of insects emerge. You
will find on rivers that the Blue Winged Olives, as an
example, often hatch best from stretches of swiftly flowing

water, mostly on warm evenings after mid summer, and that they appear in the greatest numbers after sundown. An imitation of the Blue Winged Olive is therefore likely to be most productive at this time and in these conditions.

Earlier in the evening, before the sun has set, you may find that Small Spurwings or Small Dark Olives are on the water, so you use the best imitations of these species you can find. In May and early June, Medium Olives form a large part of the fish's diet on many streams. They emerge throughout the day, possibly being joined by hatches of Iron Blues between 2 pm and 4 pm.

Similarly on some stillwaters you will see Pond Olives hatching at mid summer. You may also notice that they often fly off the surface so quickly that it is hardly worth the trout's while to pursue them. Instead, the trout may then concentrate their attention on the ascending nymphs. Sedges will flop and scutter about on the lake at nightfall, and you will sometimes detect a swirl beneath the surface, or a boil, which tells you that the fish are feeding on them. A swirl followed by a shower of leaping minnows or small coarse fish will suggest that the trout are plundering the massed shoals of tiny fish which are present in many still-waters.

Observe these things, and fish the logical method with flies to suit the occasion. Remember that no matter how closely you study artificial flies, examining the dressings and learning all the weird and wonderful names, they will mean nothing whatever to you until you have a basic knowledge of the trout's natural food. Then, matching the artificials to the natural flies, you will quickly discover that the subject is in truth a very simple one.

For myself, I have never allowed my thinking to go very far beyond the basics. Offhand I cannot tell you the dressings of more than a mere handful of standard patterns, and you will seldom meet another fisherman who can positively identify more than a dozen species of natural fly, if that. But a reasonable working knowledge of the subject certainly adds to the fascination of the sport as a whole, and at times may enable you to take a good bag of trout when you might otherwise have gone home blank.

Natural Flies and Insects

Here I give an outline of the types and names of natural flies you may most commonly see, and then, later, I list the artificial flies which from my own experience are most effective on the various types of water we have discussed. Also included are some general notes as to individual habits of the species, their distribution and hatching seasons.

1 Flies which hatch from the water
Upwinged flies, known as duns. These include:

Large Dark Olive. Known also as Large Olive or Spring Olive. A large, relatively dark grey/olive coloured fly. Hatches during the winter months, but is often present in large numbers in April and early May, and again in late September and October. Very common on rivers throughout the British Isles.

Medium Olive. Similar in appearance to the Large Dark Olive, but a little paler in colour and somewhat smaller. Widely distributed, appearing on most trout rivers from early May until the end of the season. Hatches most strongly in May, June and September during the daytime.

Pond Olive. Seen mostly on stillwaters around mid summer. Similar in appearance to the Medium Olive, although darker in colour. Quick hatching.

Small Dark Olive. Common, though somewhat localised. Abundant on many moorland streams and rain fed rivers. Sometimes ignored by trout. Hatches during the summer months, often in the late afternoon and early evening.

Blue Winged Olive. Appears throughout the season, but most in evidence on warm evenings from late June until the season ends. Hatches well in areas of broken water. Often struggles wildly in the surface while hatching. Present on most rivers throughout the British Isles. Very common.

Pale Watery Dun. A small, pale straw coloured fly, often emerging in warm sunny weather. Most prolific on chalkstreams. Very quick hatching, sometimes directly from surface weedbeds. Duns often ignored by trout.

Pale Evening Dun. Relatively large, appearing almost white. Hatches from mid-June until the end of August,

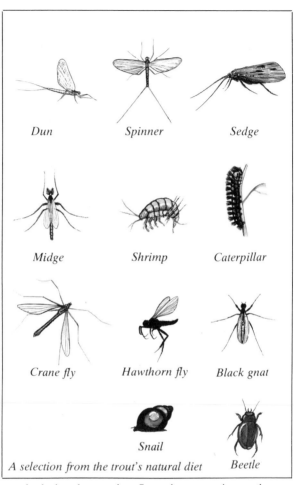

Dun

Spinner

Sedge

Midge

Shrimp

Caterpillar

Crane fly

Hawthorn fly

Black gnat

Snail

A selection from the trout's natural diet

Beetle

mostly during the evening. Sometimes remains on the surface for a considerable time before taking off, enabling the fish to sip them down at will. Prefers slower impounded water, as may be found above weirs, hatches, etc.

Iron Blue. A small, dark grey/blue fly. Hatches occur very intermittently, sometimes in quantity and mostly in wet or windy conditions. Generally, numbers appear to be in decline over recent years. May appear suddenly at any stage of the season, but most in evidence during May, June and September.

Small Spurwing. A pale fly, rather smaller than the Pale Evening Dun. Appears throughout the warmer months, especially during the early evening. Widely distributed.

Mayfly. Very large, each wing measuring perhaps an inch or more. Straw coloured body with greenish wings and three long tails. Very common, well known to fishermen and non-fishers alike. Short season, lasting perhaps three weeks, usually between mid-May and mid-June, varying from one water to another. On a few rivers, notably in Wiltshire, the Mayfly may appear at any time from mid-May until late September. The largest trout of all on lakes and rivers will rise to this insect when it is available in sufficient quantity. Strongest hatches often occur between 3 pm and 6 pm.

Yellow May Dun. Not to be confused with the Mayfly, this species hatches on many waters, but seldom in large numbers. Smaller than the Mayfly and quite a bright yellow in colour. This fly is not of great importance to the fly fisherman, although it is occasionally taken.

March Brown. Another large fly common on some rain fed rivers. Appears in late March and during April, hatching especially from fast, turbulent stretches. The hatches are brief, often lasting only for a minute or two. This fly appears to have declined considerably in numbers over recent years.

Broadwing (Caenis). A tiny fly, pale in colour, sometimes known as the Angler's Curse. Hatches are often very heavy just after sunrise and sometimes late in the evening, on both lakes and rivers.

Soon after hatching from the nymph stage, the flies listed above moult, changing from duns to spinners. As spinners they can mate, and the female then goes off to lay her eggs in the water. Some species drop their eggs in a bunch, or eggball, some dip time and again onto the surface releasing a number of eggs at each touch down, while some crawl down a post or reed stem to deposit their eggs on some fixed object under water. Either way, the spinners then die and float away on or sometimes just beneath, the surface. Egg laying takes place mostly in the evenings, although you will also see some spinners on the stream in the early morning and during the daytime.

The female spinners are very different in appearance

The Life Cycle of an Aquatic Fly

Bridges, etc.

Stones/gravel

1 Eggs are laid in the water by female spinners

2 Nymphs develop, with rudimentary wing cases

3 Nymphs mature, with fully developed wing cases

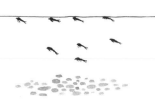

4 Nymphs come to the surface to hatch

5 Duns hatch ...   ... and become airborne

6 Duns moult, and become spinners

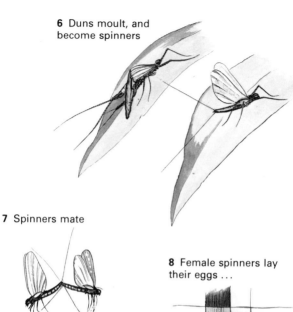

7 Spinners mate

8 Female spinners lay their eggs ...

... under water

... by dipping, releasing eggs in ones and twos

... or by 'bombing' eggballs, a cluster of eggs carried below abdomen

53

from the duns. They have changed colour, usually to a pale orange or reddish hue, with shiny transparent wings and rather longer tails. It is the females which are mostly taken by the trout as they drift downstream, the males usually having died in the meadows or along the river banks. I usually find that a single fly pattern, the Pheasant Tail, with minor variations, will suffice to represent all the spinners with the exception of the Mayfly and Broadwing.

2 Flies which hatch from the water, other than upwinged duns

Sedges. There are said to be over two hundred different species of sedge, varying a good deal in size and colour. All have their wings folded down over their relatively fat bodies while at rest, very like many of the moths. Nearly all rivers and lakes have sedge hatches, and it is a very important fly from the angler's point of view. One species or another may be present at any stage of the season, at any time of the day, and the fisherman may use a sedge pattern with success at any time. You may find, however, that the summer months are best for sedge fishing, specially at late evening.

Stoneflies. Several species of stonefly exist, varying very considerably in size and colour; they have relatively narrow wings held flat on top of the body while at rest. The large stonefly has wings measuring up to an inch or so each in length, while those of the Needle fly and the Willow fly may be approximately $\frac{1}{2}$ in long. Many of the faster flowing rain fed streams have large hatches of stonefly. Artificials are often most effective when fished across and down with considerable movement.

Reed Smuts. These are small black or dark brown insects which may be recognised by their habit of swarming in myriads near the water's edge, especially in marshy areas. There are several different species, some of which hatch out in large numbers from roots among the reed growths, while others, including the larger species, 'pop' out suddenly from the surface of the water to rest there for a moment before flying off. These are taken greedily by trout as they hatch, but the smaller ones, which may be little larger than a pinhead, are usually taken with a quiet sip as they float down upon the current. Reed Smuts appear in warm weather from May through to August, in which month smut fishing is often at its height.

Midges (Chironomids). There are many different kinds of chironomid, all with long legs and a hunched, mosquito-like appearance. These include the 'buzzers' which are becoming increasingly important to fly fishers, especially on stillwaters. Some midges have the nasty habit of settling upon the exposed parts of your anatomy and piercing the skin with their long proboscis. The 'sting' can be most irritating, as can the resultant swelling. The pupae 'hang' for some time in the surface of the water before the flies emerge, and the trout often take them in this stage. The pupae can be well imitated by 'buzzer' nymphs which hang hook down in the surface film. Chironomids are especially numerous in areas of water which carry a relatively high degree of pollutants.

3 Creatures which spend their life under water
Those of greatest interest to trout include shrimps, snails and crayfish. Trout consume many of these crustacea, which are highly nourishing and are said to account for the pink flesh of some fish. A crayfish is about the best meal a trout can get. They are not generally as easily available as snails and shrimps, however, since during daylight hours they remain hidden under any roots and vegetation along the margin, coming out at night to feed. Nor can they be successfully imitated on a small hook or fished in a conventional manner.

Most fishermen recognise the importance of an artificial shrimp today. These are often 'leaded' in the construction to make them sink, and fished near weed growths or close to the river bed, sometimes at depths of 5 ft or more. The difficulty here is detecting the take of a fish, as discussed in a previous chapter. There are few good imitations of the snail, although to me it seems likely that a convincing pattern would prove very profitable, for some species of snail are taken by trout as they float near the surface. There is room for experiment here.

4 Land bred insects
Many insects which are born on land rather than in the water, are of considerable interest to fish and fishermen

when they get onto the surface, often in a high wind. Trout take some land bred creatures well, such as caterpillars, ants, beetles, spiders, moths, crane flies, black gnats and hawthorn flies. Imitations of such insects are very useful, for the creature may 'happen' onto the stream at any time during their season in the winged stage. A difficult trout, almost uncatchable perhaps with a small dun or spinner or nymph imitation, will often grab a beetle pattern or a large bushy caterpillar as if he had been waiting for it all day, especially beneath overhanging trees or undergrowth.

Again, watch the insects which are near the water and likely to get blown onto the stream. Put a few like artificials in your fly box just in case.

This outline of the species of insects you may see is intended only as a guide. It can be no more than that, for some of the flies mentioned appear on one water but not another. Some are prolific in one particular area of the country and sparse or non-existent elsewhere. A few may be so localised as to habitat that they exist in one length yet are absent from another length of the same river. Furthermore, their density often varies greatly from one season to another.

I find that in practice you can 'prune' your list of artificial flies to a mere handful, for many of the natural flies are so similar in appearance that they can be represented by a single pattern.

Artificial Patterns

Here I include a short list of fly patterns which might be a useful initial selection for the various types of water we have discussed. You may wish to begin with these, discarding or adding to the list in time as you see fit.

Dry flies
The following standard dry flies in various sizes are likely to be productive on the majority of rivers.

Duns

Gold Ribbed Hare's Ear	Tup's Indispensable
Greenwell's Glory	Orange Quill
Blue Dun	Iron Blue
	Grey Duster

Spinners (dry)
Pheasant Tail
Lunn's Particular

Others (dry)
Caperer (sedge)
Little Red Sedge
Black Gnat
Coch-y-Bonddu

Underwater flies and nymphs
Pheasant Tail Nymph
Grey Goose Nymph
Shrimp
Corixa
PVC Nymph
Chompers
Midge Pupa
Hatching Sedge

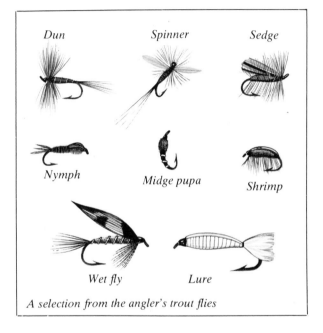

A selection from the angler's trout flies

Additional dry flies (productive on waters where the corresponding natural insect occurs)

Mayfly Dun
Spent Mayfly (Spinner)
March Brown
Hawthorn Fly

Crane Fly
Great Red Sedge
Yellow Sally

A selection of popular wet flies which in appropriate hook size may be used on most rain fed streams and stillwaters

Coachman
Butcher

Dunkeld
Alexandra

Peter Ross	February Red
Mallard and Claret	March Brown
Invicta	Gold Ribbed Hare's Ear
Zulu	Greenwell's Glory
Wickham's Fancy	Grey Duster
Poult Bloa	Spider patterns (various)
Partridge and Orange	

A selection of lures used principally on stillwaters

Baby Doll	Worm Fly
Church Fry	Sweeny Todd
Black Chenille	Muddler Minnow
Appetizer	Jersey Herd
Polystickle	Missionary
Whisky Fly	

Changing the fly – Gordon Mackie attends to the business end of his tackle (Photo © Graham Swanson)

Getting Started

So – you find yourself standing on the bank, looking at a stretch of water that falls approximately into one of the categories described in chapters 4 to 9. You possess a current rod licence and you also have a licence to fish for trout in that particular piece of water. Not only that, but you now have a glimmering of where fish may be feeding, the method you want to adopt and the kind of fly which may bring results.

If you are a beginner, you might like to run a quick check on the equipment that you will probably be using. Chapter 12 goes into more detail on choices of tackle, but this section deals with it in general terms.

The Rod

In your hand you have the rod, one which you feel is suitable for the water to be fished, bearing in mind the advice given at the ends of chapters 4 to 9. (If you've reached the water by car, you might find it convenient to tackle up in the car park. Trout anglers travel light. To get to the bankside it is a good idea to carry the rod low down, butt forward, so as not to stub it into the ground or against a tree.)

The Reel

That one is pretty obvious. But beginners may not appreciate that the trout angler makes much less use of his reel for retrieving the line than coarse or sea anglers. Once the fly is cast, the essence of trout fishing is to retrieve the line with the fingers, and it will fall in a heap around your feet (or in the boat). Try not to tread on it. Nor should you attempt to play a fish from the reel; use your fingers again.

Line

Basically the line is in four parts: (1) the backing; (2) the fly line; (3) a length of monofilament to join the fly line to (4) the leader. Items (1), (2) and (4) are described in chapter 12. Item (3), which is a length of about a yard of approxi-

mately 20 lb b.s. nylon, and is the first section of my 'manu-
factured' leader (see page 70), is generally attached to the
fly line by a needle knot, for smoother passage through the
rod rings. Leave this butt section attached to the fly line. It is
a simple matter then to tie on a fresh leader using a double
blood knot. The needle knot and blood knot are described
in chapter 12.

The Fly

This is the business end of your tackle, and the pattern you
choose is entirely your concern. You should eventually be
able to change your fly quite easily, and it is worth settling
on a good knot to tie the hook to your leader. (On many
rods, at the point where the handle begins, there is a keeper
ring, very useful for securing your fly if you are moving
around the waterside.)

That concludes this brief summary of the equipment you
need to get started. You can hardly make do without a
landing net, if you hope to land a fish of any size, and you'll
need a blunt instrument (the priest) to despatch a fish of
takable dimensions. But all this, and much else in the way of
associated equipment, is described in chapter 12. It simply
remains for you to study the following information on the
mechanics of casting, to practise casting in some wide open
space before you venture to the waterside, and to absorb the
principles of good angling behaviour in chapter 11.

Mechanics of Casting

Casting a line is very easy, but you will need to practise for a
time in order to get the knack; and if you come to trout
fishing from another branch of angling, fly casting will seem
very strange. In other techniques it is the weight at the end
of the line that propels the cast – in fly casting it is the line
itself that is the casting weight.

It is not the power of your arm which propels the line
backwards and forwards. It is the power you can get from
the rod. Assuming that you are using a line of the specified
weight for your rod, then your job is to get the timing right.
When you have mastered that, the rod will do the rest for
you. The rod acts rather like a spring, so that when its bend,
or flex, is greatest, it will propel the line at maximum speed.

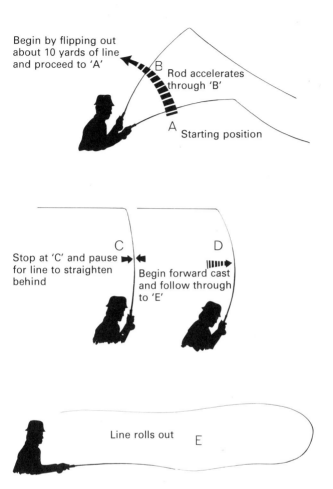

Begin by flipping out about 10 yards of line and proceed to 'A'

B Rod accelerates through 'B'

A Starting position

Stop at 'C' and pause for line to straighten behind

C

Begin forward cast and follow through to 'E'

D

Line rolls out E

Mechanics of casting

The degree of flex you obtain from the rod depends not upon the amount of force you use, but upon your arresting the movement of the butt section so that you put power into the tip of the rod. You do not always want maximum power for shorter or slower, more delicate presentation. But the degree of power, and hence the degree of rod flex and line speed, will vary according to the amount of check, or arrestation, you impart in the butt section.

It is the degree of power you impart in the back cast which largely governs the speed of delivery in the forward cast. The checking of the butt section in the back cast is therefore a vital consideration. The other crucial factor is the moment at which the rod begins its forward movement. The spring should change from a backward movement to a forward movement just as the line is fully extended to the rear. If the rod begins its forward motion too soon or too late it will lack the power to send the line forward correctly. Clearly if you allow the line to lose momentum behind you, the flex and power of the rod is reduced.

In practice, you will find that a good cast is made by 1. a positive upward movement of the forearm (A to B in the diagram); 2. a checking of the rod at a point when it is roughly vertical above your head, about 12.0–1.0 on the clock (C in the diagram); 3. a slight pause to allow the line to extend fully behind you; and 4. a smooth yet positive forward motion of the rod as you bring the forearm down to about 2 o'clock (D in the diagram).

The wrist should be kept fairly stiff, for otherwise it will allow the rod to stray too far from the vertical in the back cast, your line will lose its momentum and instead of extending sweetly it will drop behind you. This is what happens to many beginners. You then either get the fly caught up in vegetation to the rear, or if you do manage some kind of forward delivery the line lands on the water in a heap of loose coils.

Keep all movement of rod and line tight and positive. Hold a loop of line in your free hand as you cast, but hold it taut. This too will help to flex the rod and speed line movement.

---

11 Angler Behaviour

Beginners can become pretty confused on the question of etiquette, unwritten rules, and what is and is not considered sportsmanlike behaviour. All this boils down to really is

Even a big reservoir can get crowded in places
(Photo © Angling Times*)*

manners, the showing of reasonable courtesy to others who must share the water with you. It also means caring for the countryside, and treating the water and its inhabitants with respect. To many, such things are taken for granted, but it is a sad fact that some do spoil angling days for others by their thoughtless actions.

There are countless ways in which you can be guilty of poor behaviour, so here I list some of the most important points to remember.

An Angler's Country Code

1. Never leave any litter on the bank or in the water. Even a sweet wrapping should always be taken away when you leave.

2. Never drop nylon onto the ground, even short lengths. It can cause a lingering and painful death to birds and small animals. Make a twist of it, put it in your pocket and burn it when you get home.

3. Leave all gates as you find them.

4. Park your car sensibly, so as to leave room for others.

5. Never obstruct gateways.

6. Observe signs and notice boards, whether placed there by the fishery or by the farmer.

7. Try to avoid crushing bankside vegetation. This is valuable as cover and pleasing to the eye.

8. Remember that a lighted match or cigarette end can cause fire in dry conditions.

9. Take care to cause no damage to gates, stiles, huts, bridges, boats, etc.

General Courtesy

1. Never 'crowd' another fisherman. As a rough guide, for large lakes and reservoirs, try not to fish closer than about 40 yards from another angler. On small stillwaters, give him the same distance or more if conditions allow. River fishermen need more space still, depending upon the size of the stream. If, for instance, it is a small sidestream of perhaps six or seven yards in width, allow him 200 to 300 yards of unspoiled water if you can. On a very wide river he will need rather less space.

2. If for any reason you have to approach much closer than this, you should ask the other angler's permission to do so.

3. If you must approach and begin fishing – perhaps there are several rods on a confined length of river – always do so behind him, never ahead of him.

4. On narrow rivers, small stillwaters, and any other water where trout may be laying close to the bank, make sure that you always walk well away from the water so as not to frighten the fish. Do this even if no other fishermen appear to be about.

5. Boat fishermen should always leave plenty of room for those fishing from the bank, as well as keeping well clear of other boats in the area.

6. Things which you find enjoyable, such as a radio set, may be offensive to others.

7. If you are wading, please do so slowly and with extreme caution. If you do not you will 'bolt' your fish and maybe someone else's.

8. Make sure you know all the rules of the fishery and the boundaries which apply, and do please observe these at all times.

9. If any rule seems to you to be senseless or over restrictive, try to get the rule changed. Do not break the rule and then argue about it afterwards.

10. Always be courteous and friendly to everyone you meet about the water. Help them to enjoy their day as much as you hope to enjoy yours.

---

12 Fishing Tackle

Much of the pleasure of fly fishing is to be had from the ownership and use of good tackle. It need not be very expensive, but performance does depend largely upon having the right tools for the job. The rod should be long enough but not too long for the kind of water you are going to fish, the line must be of a weight which suits the rod and the conditions, and the leader should be suitable as to length, taper and strength. You will need other items such as a reel, a landing net, sensible clothing and legwear, and a fishing bag to house your fly box and the numerous bits and pieces which anglers tend to accumulate.

While it is helpful to have a wide choice of tackle, the variety available today is such as to 'blow the mind' of the beginner, so here I shall attempt to simplify your selection.

Rods

A variety of materials are used in the manufacture of fishing rods, the most common being cane, fibreglass and carbon fibre (graphite). Cane nowadays usually means 'split' cane, six long sections of split bamboo being glued together to form a rod of hexagonal cross section. Several makes of top quality cane rods are available, giving a wide choice of

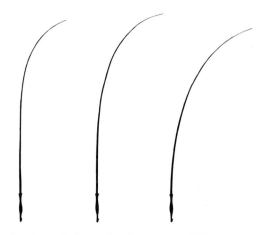

Rod actions: (left to right) tip action; middle to tip action; butt action

different 'actions', from a slow butt action, in which the rod bends throughout its length, to a stiff tip only action.

Fibreglass is a very popular material. It is strong and extremely hardwearing. These rods are generally made from hollow glass sections, they are light in use and relatively inexpensive (and the beginner can purchase a 'kit' from which to build himself a fibreglass rod).

Carbon fibre, or graphite, is a material tough enough to allow the most slender rod construction. The rods are expensive but delightful to use, even lighter than fibreglass, and are more versatile in that a wider range of line weights can be used. They are very powerful, enabling you to cast long distances with comparative ease. I feel there is room for improvement in some areas of rod design, however. Breakages appear to occur more frequently with these rods, and the ability of some to control a lively fish leaves something to be desired in my view.

Having tried all these materials, my own preference is for hollow fibreglass. I use two Hardy Fibalite rods, of 8 ft 3 in and 9 ft, and for my needs they can hardly be bettered. I would recommend hollow fibreglass as the most suitable rod material for beginners. You may find that you want to stick to it as I now do.

Lines

Most fly lines in use today are plastic coated over a plaited terylene core. The plastic is usually of a 'foamy' quality, incorporating minute bubbles, which enables the line to float to a greater or lesser degree according to design specification. Recommended line weights vary to suit the action of the rod. The weight you should use appears on the butt section of most good rods. For example, #6 means that a No. 6 line is most suitable.

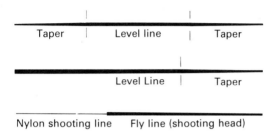

Line tapers: (top) double taper; (centre) forward taper; (bottom) shooting head

You may wish to use a floating line, a 'sink tip', a slow sinker or fast sinker. This will depend upon the kind of fishing you are going to do. A sinking line is useful for fishing the flies at depth in stillwaters, while if you are fishing mostly dry fly and upstream nymph on rivers, you are likely to find a floater more suitable. I use a floating line mostly, both for wet fly and dry fly and nymph fishing.

Fly lines have a variety of tapers. Some are thicker in the middle, tapering at each end. These are called 'double taper' lines, allowing for very delicate presentation but not designed primarily for distance casting. As one end becomes worn the line can be reversed, so that in effect it has a double life.

Forward taper or weight forward lines are thicker at the point than in the middle, allowing you to cast greater distances at the possible expense of delicacy. These lines are very useful on lakes where distance casting may be necessary, while double taper lines are generally the more popular on rivers.

'Shooting-heads', which are short sections of line, usually of 10 yards, are popular on reservoirs too. The reel contains nylon, to which the shooting head is attached, and the considerable forward weight of the line, coupled with the use of the lighter nylon line, allows you to 'shoot' prodigious distances. I find the method rather cumbersome and indelicate, and the nylon can easily tangle, but there is no doubt that far greater distance can be achieved with this method.

Many of the lines which are designed to float do not in fact do so. If they sink, perhaps only a few inches, it becomes much harder to pick the line cleanly off the water, and the fly is more likely to go under too, tending to drown the fly so that it becomes waterlogged, a nuisance if you wish to keep your fly nicely afloat on the surface. I have tried most makes of fly line and spent a considerable sum in my search for the best for my needs. Some time ago, however, I changed to the Garcia double taper de luxe floater, and am still entirely satisfied with this line. I am now using my eighth line of this make and find it excellent for general purpose work.

Reels

One of the main considerations when choosing a fly reel is to ensure that it is large enough to accommodate comfortably all of your line. If you cram a line into a reel of too small diameter it will chafe and ruin your line very quickly.

There is no need to buy an expensive reel. Even the cheapest can be perfectly serviceable, but do fit it onto the made-up rod before buying it so that you are sure its weight does not upset the balance of the outfit. Automatic reels, which wind the line back onto the spool very rapidly at the touch of a lever, are inclined to be too heavy for all but the heaviest rods in my experience, although 'geared' reels, enabling you to wind the line yourself at far greater speed than with a conventional reel, can be a distinct advantage.

I like to have two or three reels with me, or one reel with interchangeable spools, so that it becomes a simple matter to change line weights or use one of a different taper should conditions alter during the day. You may have to cast into a strong wind during the day perhaps, in which a line with more 'punch' will be useful, but you may wish to use a lighter line, possibly allowing for more delicate presentation when the wind drops at evening.

Leaders

Leaders are normally tapered to ensure that they extend correctly on the forward cast, that is, so that the thinner end, to which the fly is attached, turns nicely over at the completion of the cast. They can be purchased in tackle shops, the taper either having been produced by the tying together of lengths of nylon, or in knotless form. Knotless tapered leaders are expensive, but they do allow smooth, tangle-free casting. The butt section of many of these leaders are too fine for my liking, however. With a No. 5 plastic line I prefer the butt section to be of at least 18 lb to 20 lb breaking strain (b.s.), minimising the risk of too narrow a loop while cast-

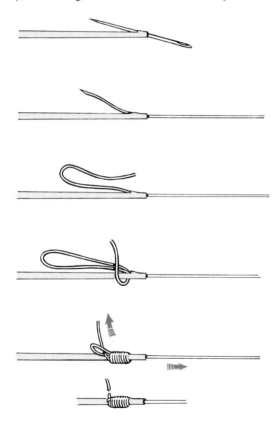

Needle knot

ing, which can cause the fly repeatedly to strike the line.

These days many fishermen tie up their own leaders from spools of different thickness. Mine are made up roughly as follows: 2–3 ft of 20 lb b.s., one foot each of 15 lb, 12 lb, 10 lb, 8 lb, 6 lb, and 4 lb, and 2–3 ft of 3 lb b.s. at the point. The final three links of nylon may be varied to suit the conditions; shorter in windy weather perhaps, longer on a calm evening. The point should be changed to a stronger nylon if you are using a large fly which might weaken the point knot, or where especially big fish are a possibility. On lakes I often change to 7 lb b.s. without altering the general make-up of the leader. The heavier sections towards the butt remain in position for the lifetime of the line, and may in fact be transferred intact when it becomes necessary to change to a new line.

Backing Line

It is advisable to attach a length of 'backing' to your casting line. This is usually made of fine terylene and is wound onto the reel before the casting line, giving it a 'base' on the reel drum. Backing line gives added length should a heavy fish strip out all your main line. The length used will be limited by the capacity of your reel, and for this reason I normally tie on just a short backing of 10–15 yards for most of the rivers I fish. On lakes where really big trout are in prospect, however, it may be advisable to use a longer length, perhaps 20–30 yards.

Waders

Fishermen usually wear either knee length boots or thigh waders. Chest waders are worn by a very few, normally on big rivers where long casting for salmon is necessary. I prefer thigh waders for my fishing, on all waters and under all conditions, even in dry weather when I have no intention of getting into the water. They are light and comfortable to wear, enabling you to kneel on a muddy bank or stand in a bog to net out your fish, and they protect your legs from all the undergrowth and tall grasses you are likely to encounter.

Waders should be hung upside down in a dry place when not in use. Special clips are available in tackle shops for this purpose. These days waders are becoming very expensive, and some tend to perish quickly, lasting perhaps only two or three seasons. Heavier makes, such as Hoods, are the most hard wearing, but they are not as comfortable as some others, I find, like the excellent Keenfisher and Streamfisher waders by Uniroyal.

Fishing Bags

A number of excellent fishing bags are available today, some of which are large and rather expensive. I like one that is relatively small, yet big enough for the few items I carry, and any fish I may catch. You should make sure that the shoulder strap is adjustable to the length you require, for it is most irritating to have it slung at the wrong level on your person, especially if it is too high. Some fishing bags have a detachable rubber lining for your catch. I prefer to use a plastic bag, one which does not leak, for the linings need to be washed thoroughly and the rubber can crack up within a short time.

These, together with sensible outdoor clothing, are the main items you will need. Additional items of tackle may include some of the following.

Other Tackle

Fly boxes. These should be large enough to house your flies comfortably without crushing them. Some of those for sale today are very expensive, but I find that cheap plastic boxes are quite adequate. For lures and wet flies there are very nice fly wallets available which are relatively inexpensive.

Line tray. Strapped to the waist, these trays are very useful, on lakes especially, for gathering in loose line as you retrieve.

Polaroid glasses. These cut out glare, and enable you to spot trout more clearly in certain conditions.

Disgorger. A scissors-type tool with serrated points for removing the hook from a fish's jaw.

Torch. Useful for changing flies in near darkness and for finding your way back to the car at night.

Priest. Loaded at one end, this tool is necessary for despatching your trout with a sharp blow at the back of the head.

Spools of nylon to replace links on the leader.

Further items may include:
>Line floatant
>Fly floatant
>Fuller's-earth
>Multi-purpose knife
>Scissors
>Spring balance

... and don't forget your permit and Water Authority Licence!

Do take care of your fishing tackle. We get into some wet and muddy old places, and this can spell death to your fly line and cause rust in fly hooks. Your rod should always be wiped down and returned to the rod bag after a day's fishing. Your line should be cleaned down regularly with a damp cloth and wound carefully back onto the reel. By taking reasonable care, you can add considerably to the life of your tackle.

Blood knot. Of the many knots used by fishermen there is one, known as the blood knot, which should be learned at the very outset. Yet it is surprising how many anglers there are who do not know how to tie it. Each fishing day you will need to change flies or tie on fresh sections of nylon, so do practise this simple knot.

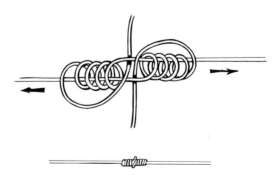

Double blood knot

This chapter has provided a brief guide to categories of equipment that the beginner should know about. If you have already handled a rod and line, or ideally have learned to cast before you purchase your own tackle, the choice will be easier. Failing that, try to get an experienced fisherman to guide you. If you possibly can, try out the tackle on grass or water before you decide which outfit to buy.

Do not be rushed into making your decision. Take your time, and remember it is better to wait, even if you are disappointed that you can't go fishing right away, than to buy tackle which is unsuitable.

Later, of course, you may wish to have a wider selection, a variety of fly lines and different leaders, than those mentioned in this chapter and elsewhere. You may choose to buy a more expensive cane or carbon fibre rod. As your experience increases, so will your capacity for the proper selection of tackle.

---

13 Fly Tying

Fly tying as an art is a rapidly evolving one, largely as a result of the vast increase in the number of waters which are now fished for trout. All the time we are finding out new information about food items which figure in the diet of trout, and discovering new materials with which to imitate them. The old standard patterns devised by anglers a hundred years and more ago are still used by many, and they catch fish as they ever did. But one of the exciting things about modern fly dressing is that the new patterns, and the new ways we have of fishing them, enable us to catch fish in circumstances which would have been considered hopeless hitherto.

When I started fishing, and that was not so very many years ago, I can recall how frustrating it was to see big trout feeding on shrimps at considerable depths, or breaking the surface when not a single fly was to be seen on the water. I felt so helpless. Now I know how to construct lifelike shrimp imitations and fish them deep down to visible fish, and I know that on occasion trout, although appearing to rise at nothing at all, are actually taking midge pupae suspended in the surface film.

As fly fishing techniques develop and our knowledge increases, so fly dressing skills improve. I would urge those taking up the sport today to study the subject of natural flies and their imitation, so that you can discover nature's secrets for yourself and copy for yourself those delicate insect forms. You may not begin to dress your own flies right away, but I hope you will in due course, for it is such a fascinating and absorbing art, almost a hobby in its own right.

There is nothing very difficult about tying a fly. The ones I tie are so simple that almost anyone could turn out a passable copy after a few minutes of basic instruction. I remember a lady friend of mine tying a fly with no instruction at all, and the following week I went out and caught a trout with it!

The beginner can do no better than obtain an instruction book such as those available from John Veniard Ltd, 4–6 High Street, Westerham, Kent TN16 1RF, which include some popular fly dressings and full details of how to tie them. There is a very helpful book in the same series as my own, *Fly Tying for Beginners*, by Geoffrey Bucknall, published by Ernest Benn. That volume is a progressive introduction to the subject.

You will need certain tools, such a a vice, hackle pliers for winding on the hackle at the head of the fly, scissors, a couple of needles, and of course the materials themselves. These will include herls and furs of various kinds for making the body of the fly, hackle feathers, tying silks, and varnish. It might be best to buy a kit which will contain everything you need to start tying your own flies. You can add further materials to your stock as you progress. Veniards can supply all such requisites, and many other suppliers advertise in the angling journals.

---

14 Further Reading

The number of books devoted to the subject of fly fishing is almost endless. I have read only a tiny proportion, although among them have been many of the classics of angling literature. I am fortunate to have a small collection of my own, and I know the enormous amount of pleasure that a good angling book can bring. Indeed, and here I repeat what has been written before, 'the next best thing to fishing is reading about it'. How very true that is.

In recommending further reading, I am passing on titles in two sections. First those which for me have been especially enjoyable, and second the works which in my own view are some of the best of what might loosely be described as 'instructional' in a general way. There will be omissions, of course, but then I can only suggest a very few of all the good works which have been written.

Pleasurable Reading

Fly Fishing: Sir Edward Grey
Fishing Dreams: T. T. Phelps
A Fisherman's Methods and Memories: Walter Barrett
Where the Bright Waters Meet: H. Plunket-Green
Trout from the Hills: Ian Niall
A Summer on the Test: J. W. Hills
A History of Fly Fishing: J. W. Hills
The Way of a Trout with a Fly: G. E. M. Skues
Fisherman's Diary: Oliver Kite
Reflections on a River: Howard Marshall
The Angler's Weekend Book: Taverner and Moore
Angler's Bedside Book: M. Wiggin

Books of rather more instructional nature

Stillwater Fly Fishing: T. Ivens
Flydresser's Guide: J. Veniard
Nymph Fishing in Practice: Oliver Kite
Fishing for Lake Trout: Conrad Voss Bark
Rough Stream Trout Flies: Taff Price
Reservoir Trout Fishing: Bob Church
Fishing the Dry Fly: Dermot Wilson

Trout Fly Recognition: John Goddard
Trout Flies of Stillwater: John Goddard

One further book I would recommend to those of a more scientific nature is

The Trout: W. E. Frost and M. E. Brown

---

15 Conclusion

Fishing is not simply a useful form of exercise, a mere recreation. It is a sport, and in any true sport there must be an element of chance, in which the quarry has as high a prospect of retaining his freedom as the hunter has of catching him. If results are assured, then it is no longer sport. It becomes butchery, killing for the sake of killing.

If you were invited to fish in a stock-pond heavily populated with big trout you would assuredly have the most successful day in terms of results that you ever had or were ever likely to have. But would you enjoy it? Could it be considered a good day's sport? There are some who would say 'yes' to both of these questions. Their catch would be of considerable commercial value, and they would be able to display their kill to admiring friends and relatives, receiving praise from many quarters. The angling press would be keen to splash the news across their pages, and the killing fly would doubtless become the rage. They might even go into the record books, ranking with the all time greats!

But fly fishing, if it is to be a sport, can have nothing to do with commercial gain, the sensationalism of the press, or fierce competitiveness. The true gain is the satisfaction of knowing that you have met a challenge fairly, and that it is your skill which has enabled you to overcome that challenge. Some angling incidents are indeed sensational, but you contain these within your own being, for who can truly relate the deepest emotions we felt at the time without leaving half of the thrill and joy untold. Competitiveness between anglers who partake for the sake of competition has no place in our sport. You compete, but the conflict is between a man and his trout, a very personal and intimate affair. You detect the whereabouts of your fish, and you stalk him, watching for his movements to decide how best to tackle him. You present your fly, mindful that your chances are slim. And when you have hooked your trout, played him and finally netted him, then you feel the real satisfaction of the sport. Whether you return the fish to the water or not, you have savoured the true spirit of hunting trout with the fly.

One of the most successful anglers I know sets himself a personal size limit of 2 lb on rivers, and even these he returns unless he has a need to keep them. Another is concerned only about killing his limit of six trout every time he goes out. He likes to keep his deep-freeze well stocked. The former, I believe, obtains so much more enjoyment from the sport, for he feels no sense of pressure when he is fishing, only peace and the knowledge that he is alone and close to nature.

To many, fishing is a form of escapism, but more and more these days we find that conditions by the water are not so dissimilar to those from which we are trying to escape. Many fisheries suffer encroachment of some kind, whether it be building development, new road projects, or as a result of increasing demand for recreational facilities. The angler sometimes has to fish in areas where boating takes place, or where families gather with children and dogs on a summer's day, adorning the countryside with their sandwich wrappings and empty cans.

Even the waters themselves are becoming increasingly threatened by such perils as pollution, and land drainage, in which the bed of a stream may be torn asunder, often apparently for no good reason. This kind of work is usually undertaken by the Water Authorities, who supposedly care for our fishing interests, as is water abstraction, which is potentially the most dangerous practice of all.

At the present time most of our fisheries are in good condition, but we should never close our eyes to the threat which exists, nor forget that many rivers which once provided wonderful fishing have been killed by the very horrors which I have mentioned. They are now fishless, so foul that no water creature of any kind can live there any more.

We must resist most strongly all proposals which may spoil the quality of our glorious sport. Do everything you can to preserve our fisheries during your lifetime, and for future generations of fly fishermen.

Index